# Approaching Ballet Anew:

## Using Resistance Bands to Explore Ballet Technique

Lisa Thorngren, MFA

ISBN: 978-1-257-99672-8

The author shall not be held liable or responsible for any injury allegedly arising from any information or suggestion in this book. Please consult your physician or health care professional before beginning any type of physical exercise.

## Table of Contents

# Introduction

There are a myriad of approaches to the teaching of ballet technique; some of them codified, and others developed through years of trial and error. As teachers, we constantly evaluate and reevaluate the effectiveness of our pedagogical methods, as seen through the improvements of our dancers. When we find a method or strategy that helps our students, we keep it and explore the idea further. The resistance-band method detailed in this book is one successful strategy. Unlike most uses of resistance bands, in which the band is used as a conditioning tool, here, the band is used to highlight and make tangible aspects of ballet technique.

As I discuss later, I have developed this method through trial and error over many years, with each subsequent class a bit more focused and ultimately more successful. I have had numerous students over the years who have commented how in one single class, their understanding of ballet technique increased dramatically. More specifically, they mention their increased ability to apply abstract technical concepts to their movement. Though they may have already had the intellectual knowledge regarding these concepts, this is often the first time they are able to gain the kinesthetic knowledge. This improvement is also visibly apparent. The students' movements look different; they are more coordinated, more dynamically balanced, and students' upper bodies are actively engaged in the movement.

Through teaching this resistance-band ballet class to my own college students, as well as others at the American College Dance Festival, I have seen how this technique can truly benefit dancers of all levels. It is my hope that the information that follows will help you to experience the benefits of working with resistance bands, and will allow you not only to increase your own understanding of ballet technique, but your students' understanding as well.

## Background

This resistance-band approach to ballet technique pedagogy began in graduate school in an MFA program in Dance; I was taking a contemporary ballet class from Dr. Cynthia Roses-Thema in which we explored ideas of dynamic alignment, whole body integration and tensegrity. Cynthia's ideas, and her own SPINE theory*, had already completely changed the way I approached ballet technique. I began to think more holistically about my body as it moved, and began finding connections between distal points on my limbs.

This process was anything but easy, however. It is one thing to understand an abstract concept of how my left fingers relate to and affect my right leg while performing a développé à la seconde (for example), but it is a separate challenge to apply that mental understanding to the physical movement. Though I ultimately met these challenges with some level of success, the process took time.

During my last year of graduate study, a colleague of mine and I were asked to substitute for one of Cynthia's ballet classes. In preparing for this class, I had the idea to use resistance bands to provide a physical, tangible connection between different parts of the body. We created a few exercises using the bands, taught a successful class, and that was the beginning of this new approach to ballet technique.

Since those few beginning exercises, I have continued to explore new ideas and new ways of utilizing the band. I always refer back to our original thoughts: that the band allows us to take an abstract concept and make it tangible. Thus, in developing new exercises, I first think about what abstract concepts we often work on or teach our students. Then, I find a way to use the band to give students a physical application of these concepts. Though it is still a challenge for students to apply a new idea to their movement, I find that the process becomes a bit easier for them, as they are better able to feel and sense this new idea, rather than merely thinking about it.

*For more information about Cynthia and her SPINE movement strategies, please visit www.thesomaticpen.com, or email her directly at Cynthia.Roses-Thema@asu.edu.

## How to Use This Book

The following two sections, "Resistance Band Use" and "Class Structure," each give valuable information to help you in teaching a resistance-band ballet class:

- "Resistance Band Use" discusses the particular resistance bands that need to be used in order for the exercises to be effective. In addition, it details the ways that the band is held, with rationale for each and how each enhances ballet technique.

- "Class Structure" gives information regarding how the class itself is set up to best facilitate use of the resistance band, and to best improve students' understanding. To truly get the most out of this experience for you and your students, please follow these guidelines.

After reading through the above-mentioned sections, you will then come to the descriptions of exercises used in class. For each exercise, such as battement tendu, there is first a discussion of how and why the resistance band is used in a specific manner for the given exercise. Then, a sample exercise, including counts and photographs (when appropriate), is given that is a representation of the movement I usually teach. Any additional information and suggestions for the sample exercise may follow.

I encourage you initially to follow the exercise exactly as I have described it. This will allow you to experience what my students experience as they use the resistance band, and will give you a deeper understanding of the role the band plays in improving ballet technique. Once you have explored these exercises and understand how the band can be used, you may find that new or modified ways of using the band also enhance your and your students' knowledge; feel free to expand upon my ideas and movements.

## How to Use This Book

# Resistance Band Use

## Choosing the Band

When I first began working with a resistance band in this manner, I used black Thera-band® resistance bands. Over time I came to realize that this strong resistance provided a little too much of an upper body workout, preventing me and many of my dance students from focusing primarily on the technical ideas being explored, and I have since switched to blue Thera-Band® resistance bands.

When choosing what length and type of resistance band to use, here are a few suggestions:

- The bands must be long enough to stretch from a dancer's left foot to right hand (with the band passing across the back) when in first arabesque at ninety degrees on the right leg. This position should not be difficult to maintain, but there should be tension in the band, and the dancer must be able to feel a solid, strong connection between foot and hand.

- The bands must have enough resistance to provide some support between the limbs in the position described above. At the same time, when the dancer is holding the band along the back with the arms in second position (see Figure 1), this position should provide some work for the arms and upper body, without completely fatiguing the dancer.

    - In my experience, a blue Thera-band® resistance band, or a band of similar resistance, does the above well.

## Using & Holding the Band

There are several ways in which the resistance bands are used/held throughout the class, each of which can be found in the figures that follow:

- *Back hold*
  The first (Figure 1) uses the resistance band with the arms in second or first (middle fifth) position. It is important that the band pass across the back and *under* the elbows, before coming up to the hands from below (Figure 2). This use of the resistance band is helpful in the following ways:

  - In order to maintain second position of the arms, the dancer is forced to reach out actively through the arms and keep them lengthened, thus finding a sense of energy and length in this position.

  - At the same time the dancer is lengthening her arms out, the band is providing a tangible connection of the arms into the back, thus reinforcing the idea of the arms being supported from and connected to the back. It is nearly impossible in this position for the arms to become disconnected from the back and the rest of the body, unless the tension in the band is completely released.

When the dancer then releases the resistance band and places the arms in second position without the band, the result is lengthened, yet connected, arms that have a sense of energy and support.

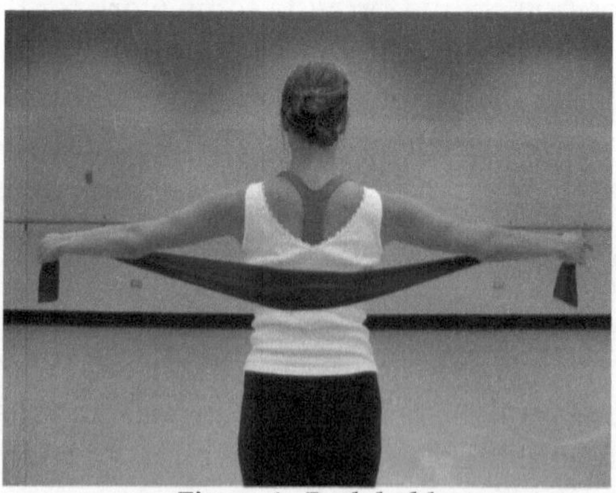

**Figure 1. Back hold**

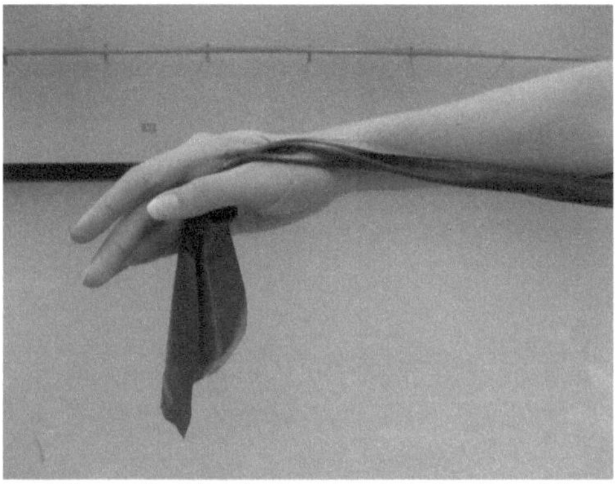

**Figure 2. Hand placement in back hold**

- *Front hold*
  The second (Figure 3) uses the resistance band with the arms in first (middle fifth) or high fifth position. The band is merely held in each hand, thus completing the circle of the arms. Depending on the exercises, I might suggest to students that they wrap the ends of the bands around their hands, so as not to have the ends swinging around. In this position, it is important that there is a small amount of tension in the band in between the hands. This use of the resistance band is helpful in the following ways:

  - By creating and maintaining some tension in the band, the arms are resisting each other slightly. This engages the upper back muscles and provides a muscular connection of the arms into the rest of the body.

  - By connecting the hands in this way, the position of the arms is more easily felt. I find that this position can be especially useful for dancers when doing chaînés, as it becomes very obvious when the arms try to pull apart or work at different heights. Dancers then become very aware of what their arms are doing when they turn, which can be difficult to sense otherwise.

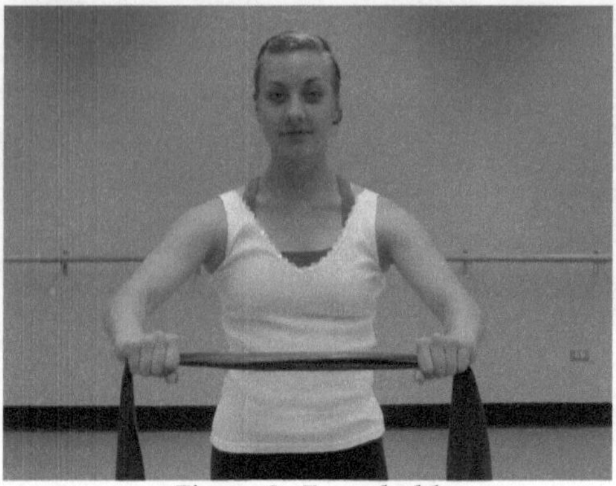

**Figure 3. Front hold**

- *Hand-to-foot*
  The third (Figures 4 & 5) uses the resistance band as a connector between a foot and a hand. Before beginning class, I have students tie one end of the resistance band in a double knot around the arch of their foot; while we do not use the resistance band in this manner until later in class, it saves us from stopping later. Some students also find the loop helpful to hold onto (or to slide their thumb into) when using the band in a back hold. In the hand-to-foot use of the band, the band can be held by the contralateral hand (the hand on the side opposite to the foot; i.e. right hand, left foot), or by the ipsilateral hand (the hand on the same side as the foot). Both methods are useful for different exercises and ideas, as we will discuss later. This use of the resistance band is helpful in the following way:

    - We are often told, as dancers, to feel connections between different parts of our bodies, but sometimes these connections are difficult to sense internally. By using the resistance band in this way, dancers can find a tangible, physical connection between distant parts of their bodies. They more easily and quickly sense a whole-body connection in movement, rather than thinking of the arms and legs separately. This also leads to a better sense and use of counterbalancing within the body.

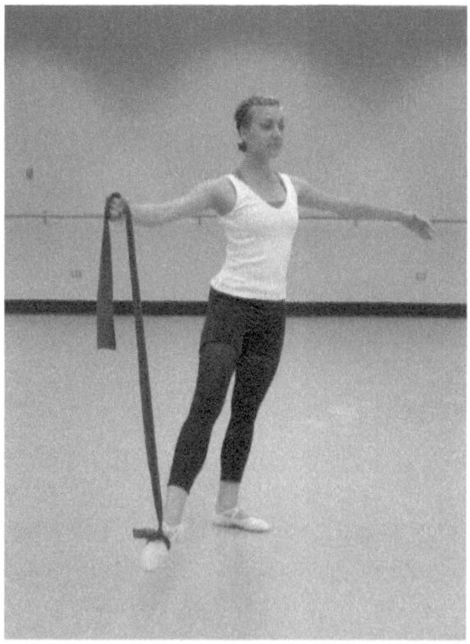

**Figure 4. Hand-to-foot hold, ipsilateral**

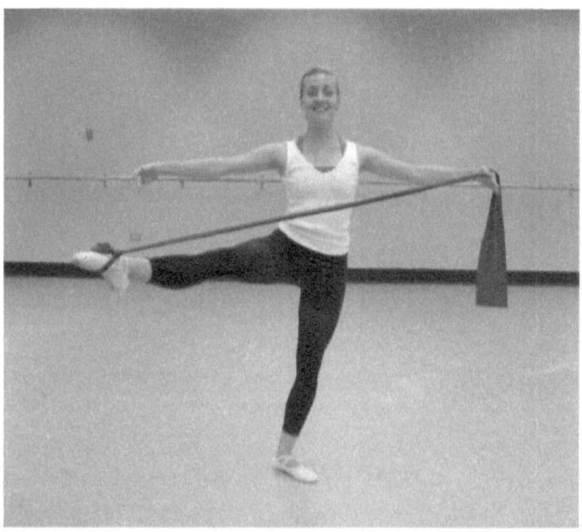

**Figure 5. Hand-to-foot hold, contralateral**

There are a few other ways in which the resistance band is used for specific exercises, but those will be explained later as we encounter them.

## Class Structure

There are several ways in which this class differs from other ballet classes we may have taught or experienced, but each of these differences serves to enhance the students' experiences and growth potential during the class.

- *Center Barre*
  Use of the resistance bands necessitates doing all of the barre exercises in the center, so that both hands can be free to hold the band. This also ensures that the dancer is using the entire upper body as a whole.

- *No Mirror*
  When I teach this class I have students face away from the mirror for two very specific reasons.

  - This class is based on the idea of sensing connections in the body, not trying to see them in the mirror. With a visual reflection of ourselves in front of us, it can become very easy to rely on the mirror to provide information about our bodies. However, to truly experience the insights and connections the resistance band can provide, it is necessary to feel from the inside out, rather than see only the outside.

  - Some of the positions and movements with the resistance band have the potential to look awkward or silly to students new to this practice; therefore it is important to remove opportunities for them to see themselves with the band so as to not distract them from their movement and learning.

- *Forget Square*
  For the purposes of sensing connections throughout the body, I strongly encourage students to forget the idea of being "square" - shoulders over hips, both pointing straight forward. In many of the exercises that follow, it is through <u>not</u> being "square" that students are able to sense the

strongest connection between the upper and lower body; they are then able to recall and reproduce this connection later, even when in positions which appear to be "square."

- *Forget Perfect Arms*
  Especially with the arms in second position, I encourage students not to feel as though this position must be perfectly held. Instead, I recommend that students continue to stretch through the entire arm without locking it, thus producing a lengthened, yet energized upper body. Also, some students have found that externally rotating the arms (so the elbows point down and palms scoop upward) helps them better sense the engagement of the upper back and the connection of the arms to the rest of the body while holding the resistance band. Regardless, it is not necessary (and may prove to be a hindrance) to have classically-correct positioning of the arms.

- *Repetition*
  Every exercise (excluding pliés) that we do in class is done first with the resistance band, and then is repeated immediately afterward without the band. This allows the dancers to immediately apply their sensations and discoveries with the band to the same movement without the band, thus providing them the opportunity to find their own way of maintaining these connections and sensations without the tangible help of the band.

- *Discussion*
  Periodically throughout the class I will pause between exercises and ask students for their comments and experiences. I find that providing students an opportunity to reflect verbally on what they have just experienced helps them better internalize and solidify their understanding. In addition, the insights dancers share often serve to help others in the class achieve the same understanding. At the end of the class I ask the students to discuss their overall experiences and discoveries.

# Exercises

## Plié

### Purpose of the Resistance Band

During pliés, I often see several things happening among my students: the arms and legs are acting separately, perhaps moving together, but not with a sense of connection; there is little energy within the movement itself; and the energy seems concentrated primarily in the lower body. Using the resistance band in a front hold, dancers will be able to sense the connection of the arms into the back, and will then be able to use the arms in the same way that the legs are being used in a plié; as the legs and knees expand into space on the way down, so do the arms. There is a sense of expansion and length through the whole body.

Though I have not yet explored this option, using the band in a back hold and moving the arms in traditional pathways during pliés would, I am sure, also provide insights for the dancers.

This exercise also acts as an introduction to the resistance band and how it feels in movement; as such, and due to time constraints, we often will not repeat this exercise without the band.

### Sample Phrase

Begins in second position en face, band in a front hold.

| Count | 1 - 2 | 3 - 4 | 5 - 8 |
|---|---|---|---|
| Movement | Demi plié (Figure 6) | Demi plié | Grand plié (Figures 7-9) |

| 1 | 2 | 3 |
|---|---|---|
| Demi plié | Remain in plié, lift the heels | Extend the legs |

| 4 - 6 | 7 - 8 |
|---|---|
| Balance on demi-pointe | Change Positions |

These sixteen counts are repeated in first position and fifth position with the right foot devant, and then the entire set begins again, bringing the left foot devant into fifth position.

**Additional Information and Suggestions**

- The arms on the demi pliés are not traditional; instead, as the knees bend the arms reach out in opposition in any direction (horizontally, vertically, diagonally), (Figure 6), and then return as the knees extend.

- During the grand plié, the arms begin in a modified en bas position and move through first (middle fifth) to high fifth as the body descends (Figures 7, 8 & 9). Then the arms reverse this pattern as the body ascends.

- The arms during the second eight counts can be held in first (middle fifth) or high fifth, so as to feel the connection of the arms into the rest of the body (Figures 10-12).

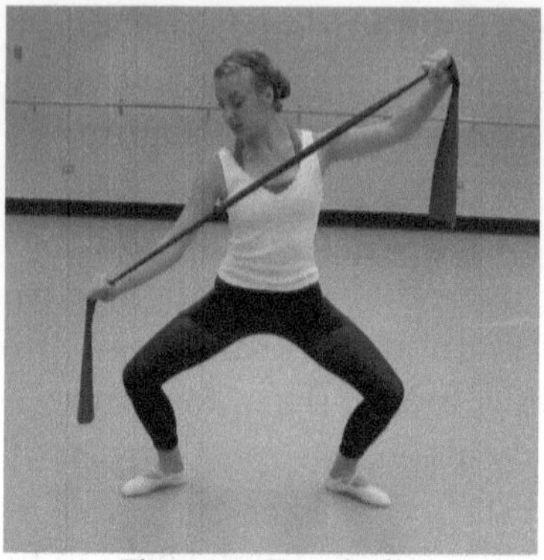

Figure 6. Demi plié

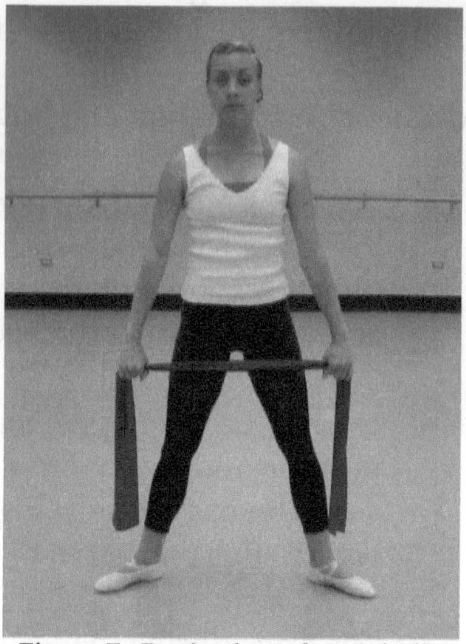

Figure 7. Beginning of grand plié

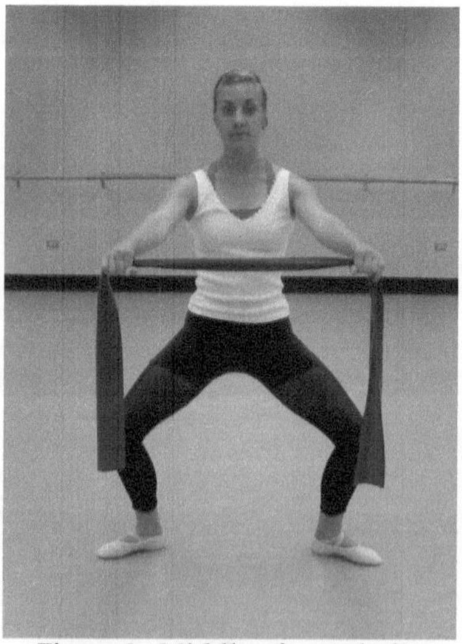

Figure 8. Middle of grand plié

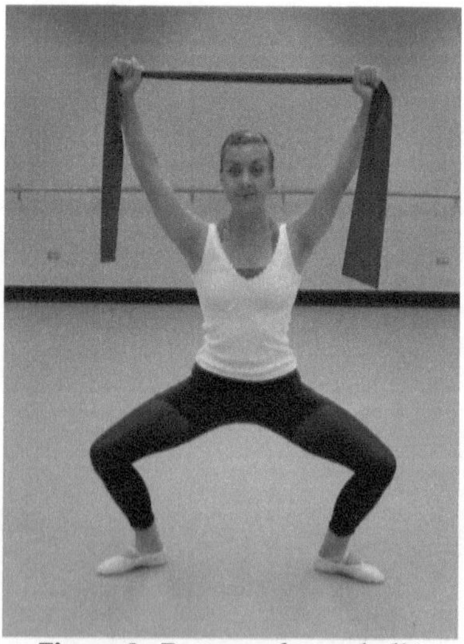

Figure 9. Bottom of grand plié

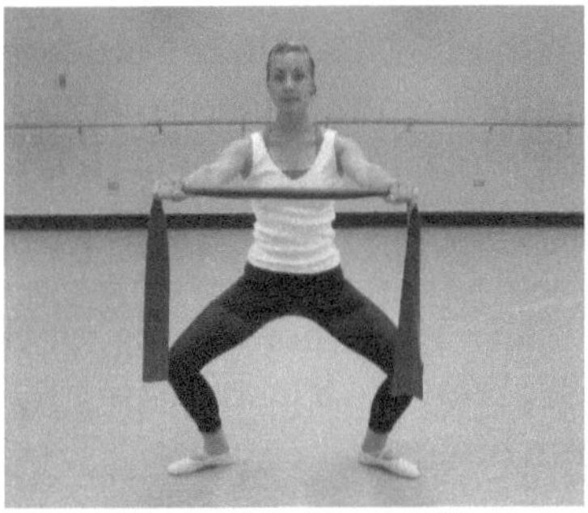

Figure 10. Demi plié

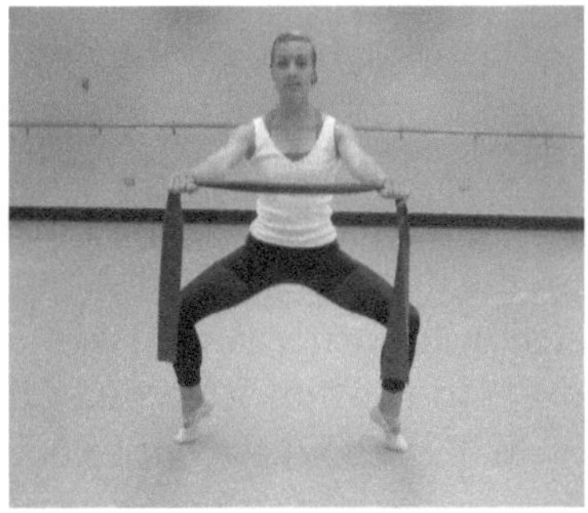

Figure 11. Demi plié with heels lifted

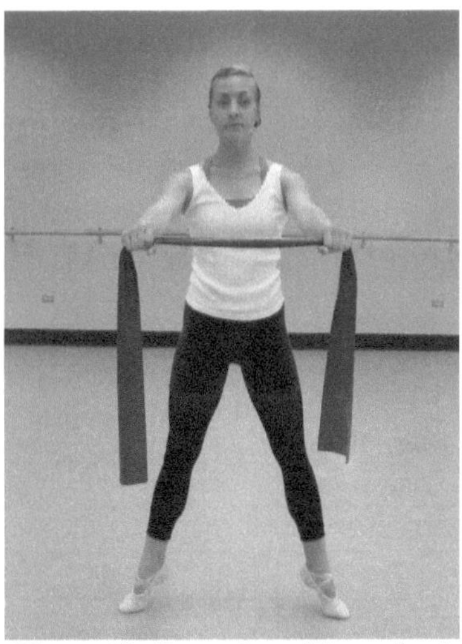

Figure 12. Second position relevé

## Battement Tendu from First Position

### Purpose of the Resistance Band

During battement tendus, as with pliés, I see in my students a disconnect between what the legs are doing and what the arms are doing. The sense of the entire body working together is lacking. By using the resistance band in a back hold, dancers can not only sense the upper body better, but they can find a sense of length and stretch in the arms as well as the spine and legs when the leg moves into a tendu. Thus, it becomes not just about the leg stretching into a tendu, but about the entire body stretching.

### Sample Phrase

Begins in first position en face, arms first position (middle fifth) with the band in a back hold.

| Count | 1 – 2 | 3 – 4 | 5 – 6 |
|---|---|---|---|
| Movement | Tendu devant, arms open to second position (Figure 13) | Close to first in demi plié, arms close to first (Figure 14) | Tendu devant, arms open |

| 7 – 8 | 1 – 2 | 3 – 4 |
|---|---|---|
| Close to first in demi plié, arms close | Tendu devant, arms open | Close to first in demi plié, arms close |

| 5 – 6 | 7 – 8 |
|---|---|
| Relevé, arms open to second position (Figure 15) | Demi plié, arms close to first |

These sixteen counts are repeated en croix, and then the entire phrase is repeated on the left side.

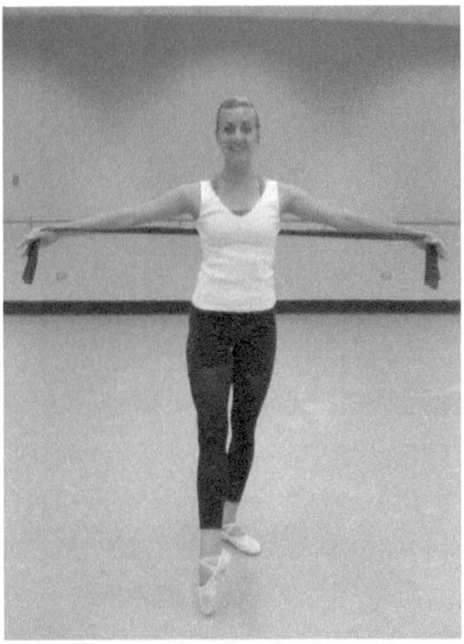
Figure 13. Tendu devant

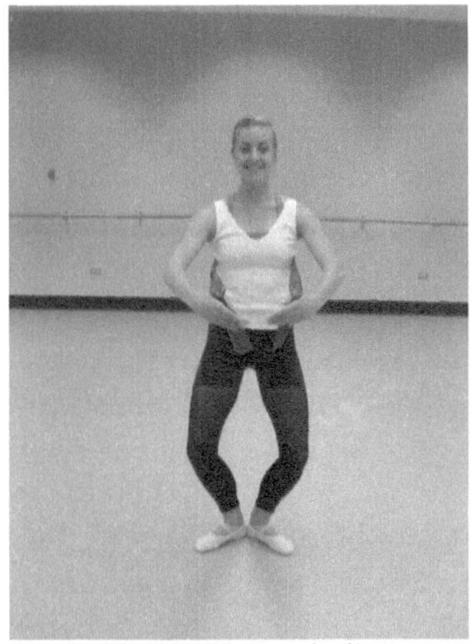
Figure 14. Demi plié

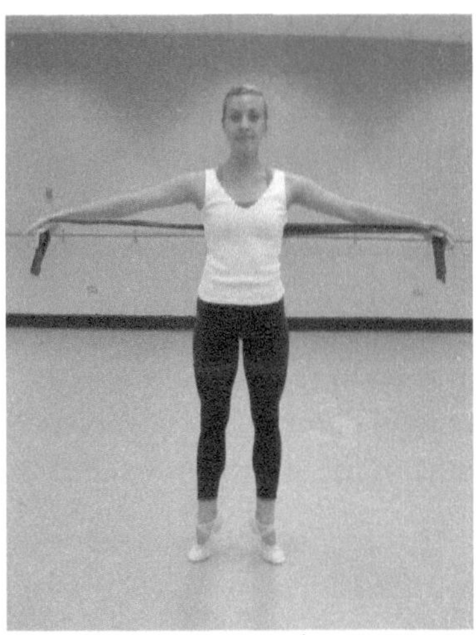
Figure 15. Relevé

## Battement Tendu from Fifth Position

### Purpose of the Resistance Band

In addition to the disconnect between the arms and legs during battement tendus addressed in the previous exercise, there is often no sense of how the torso relates to movements of the limbs. During this battement tendu exercise, we use the resistance band to explore the connections between the foot and the ipsilateral hand, and how those connections necessitate use of and energy through the torso. By using the resistance band in a hand-to-foot hold, I encourage students to feel the torso spiraling to counterbalance the working leg. Thus, when the right leg performs a battement tendu devant, the dancers should feel the torso (and the connected arms) rotating to the right (towards the leg). When the right leg performs a battement tendu derriére, the dancers should feel the torso (and the connected arms) rotating to the left (away from the leg). And as the right leg moves between directions (brushes through first position from devant to derriére, for example) the torso should feel a continuous rotation to counterbalance. Initially, I encourage students to exaggerate this movement of the torso to better sense its role in the battement tendus; ultimately, though the rotational movement itself is minimized, the sensation of engagement and energy in the torso should remain the same.

### Sample Phrase

Begins in fifth position croisé, right foot devant, arms in second position with the band in a hand-to-foot hold (Figure 16). The loop of the resistance band is around the right arch, and the end of the band is held in the right hand with some tension to start.

| Count | 1 – 4 | 5 – 8 | 1 – 4 | 5 – 8 |
|---|---|---|---|---|
| Movement | Tendu devant & close (Figure 17) | Tendu devant & close | Tendu devant, close to first position (Figure 18) | Tendu derriére, close to fifth position effacé (Figures 19 & 20) |

| 1 – 8, 1 – 8 | 1 – 2 | 3 – 4 | 5 |
|---|---|---|---|
| Reverse the previous 16 counts (tendu derriére to start) | Tendu devant | Demi-rond de jambe to écarté devant (Figure 21) | Close to fifth position croisé |

| 6 – 7 | 8 | 1 – 8 | 1 – 8 |
|---|---|---|---|
| Tendu écarté devant, close fifth position effacé | Hold | Reverse the previous 8 counts (tendu derriére to start) | Change the band to the left foot and prepare to repeat the whole exercise to the left (beginning croisé) |

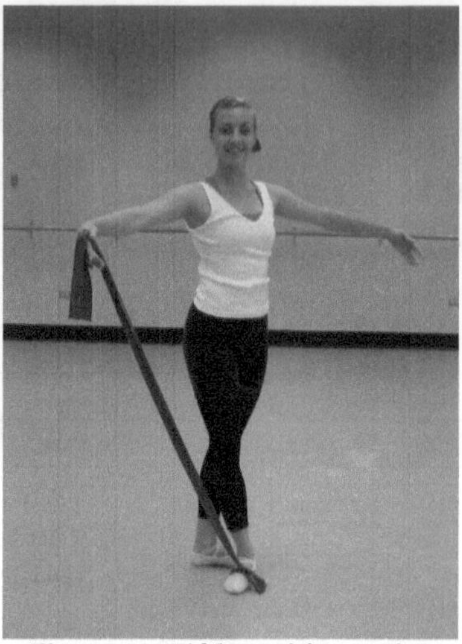

Figure 16. Fifth position croisé

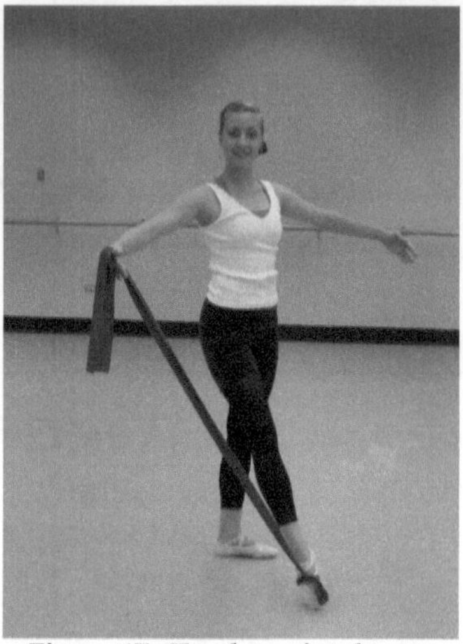

Figure 17. Tendu croisé devant

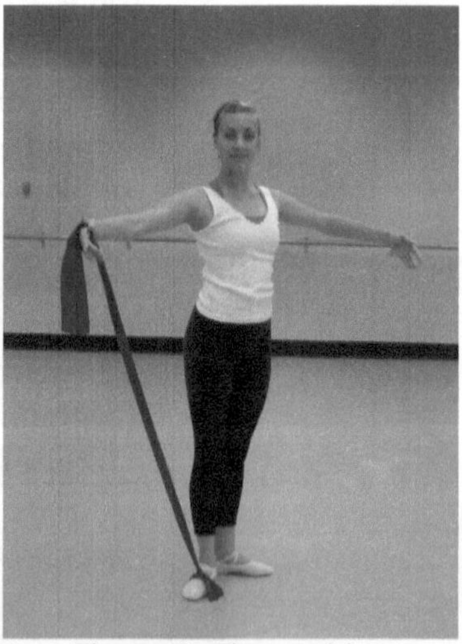

Figure 18. First position

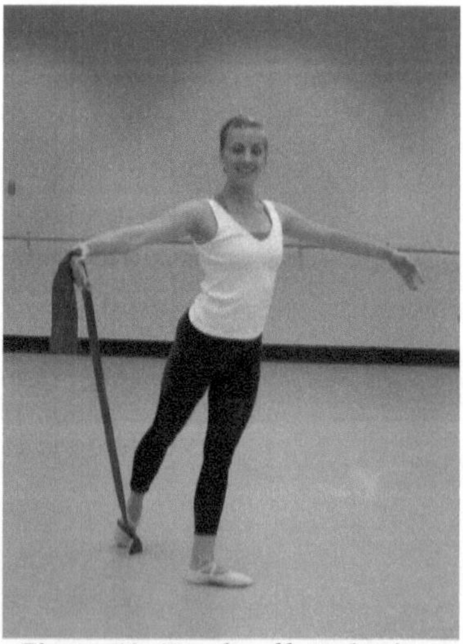

Figure 19. Tendu effacé derriére

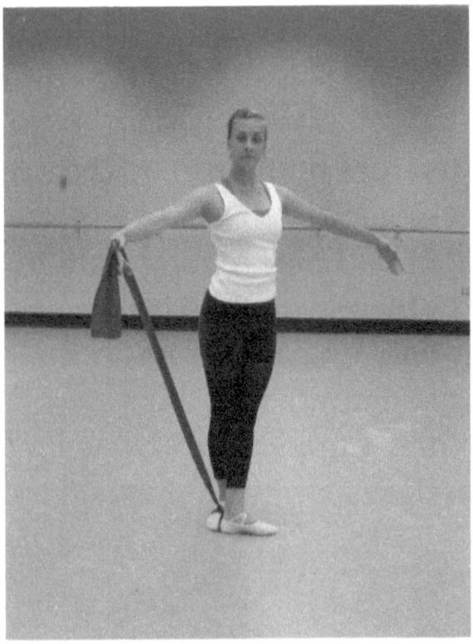

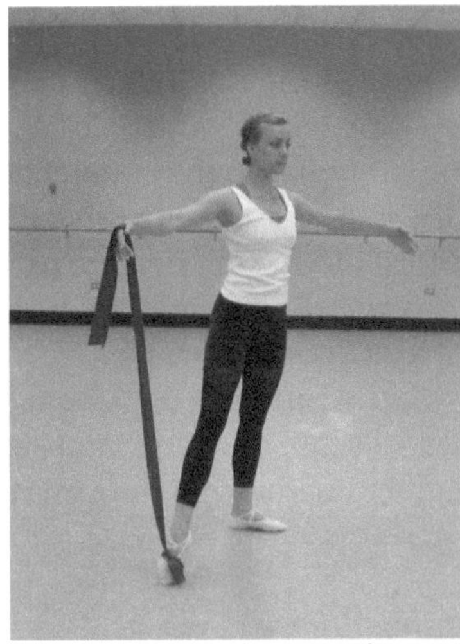

Figure 20. Fifth position effacé

Figure 21. Tendu écarté devant

As mentioned above, I will often encourage students to exaggerate the rotation of the torso to counter the leg. Such rotation in tendu devant and tendu derriére would look like the following:

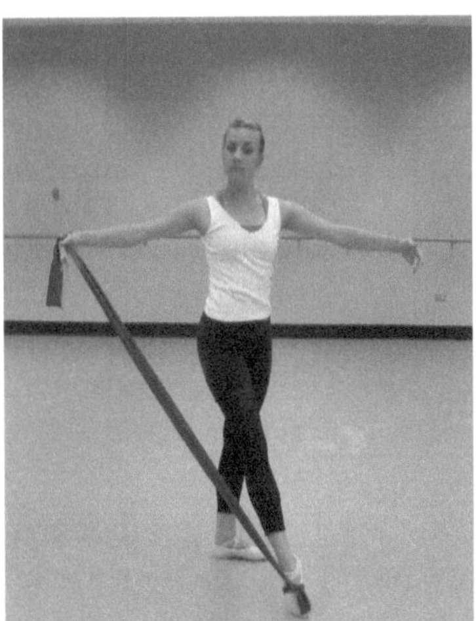

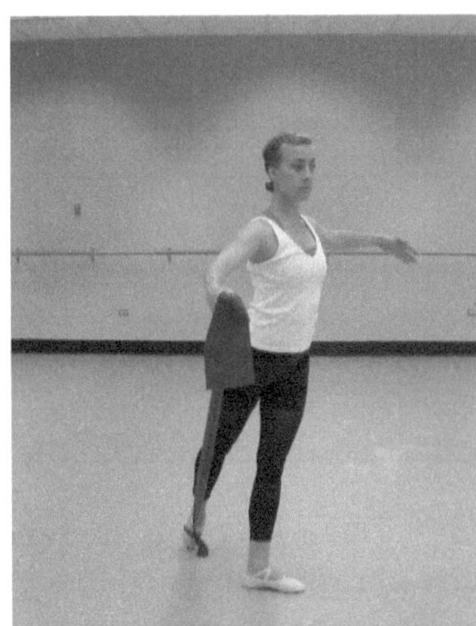

Figure 22. Tendu croisé devant, emphasizing rotation of the torso

Figure 23. Tendu effacé derriére, emphasizing rotation of the torso

## Battement Dégagé from First Position

### Purpose of the Resistance Band

Similar to the battement tendus from first position, the use of the resistance band with battement dégagés helps students understand the importance of the upper body in creating stability and support, especially as the speed of the lower body increases. Just as a tightrope walker uses a long pole for balance, using the resistance band in a back hold helps the dancers find their own internal sense of energy and stability in the upper body by actively lengthening through the arms and sending energy out beyond the fingers.

### Sample Phrase

Begins in first position en face, with the arms in second position throughout the exercise. The band is in a back hold (Figure 24). The tempo is usually variable for this exercise, beginning rather slowly, and then increasing in speed with each repetition of the exercise to challenge students' use of their upper bodies.

| Count | 1 – 8 | 1 – 8 |
|---|---|---|
| Movement | 8 dégagés à la seconde with the right leg (Figure 25) | 7 dégagés en cloche with the right leg, beginning to the front on count 1, closing to first position on count 8 (Figures 26 & 27) |

These 16 counts are repeated on the left side, and then the entire phrase is repeated (once or twice more) with an increase in speed with each repetition.

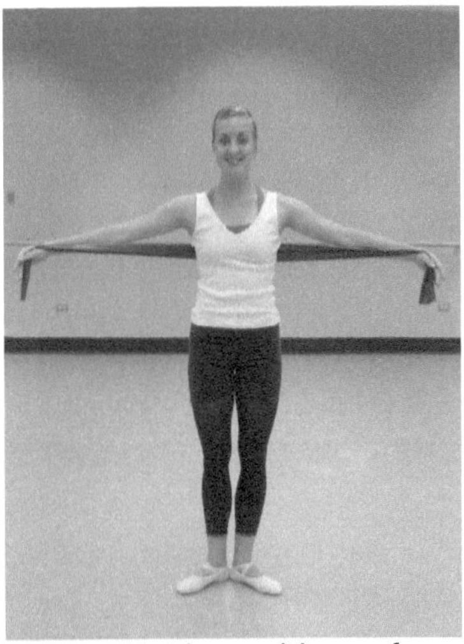

Figure 24. First position en face

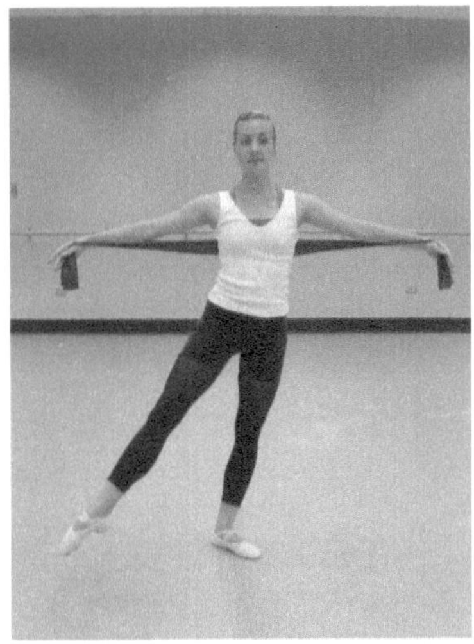

Figure 25. Dégagé à la seconde

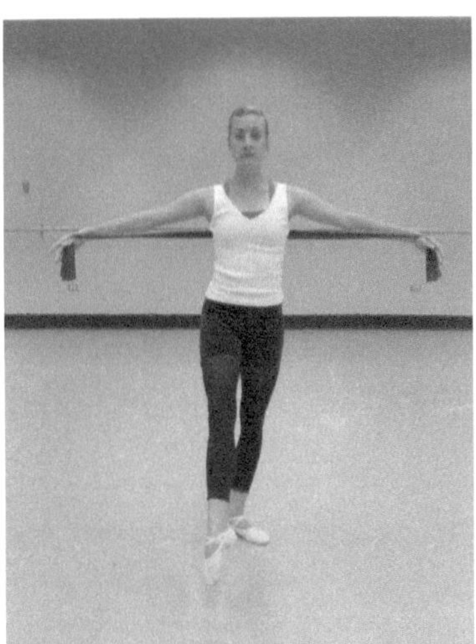

Figure 26. Dégagé en cloche

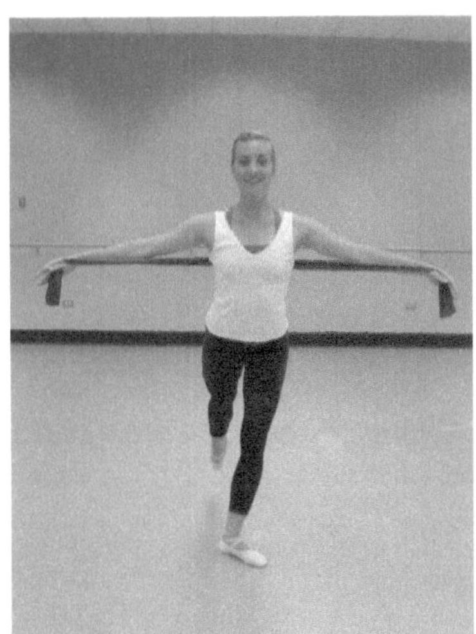

Figure 27. Dégagé en cloche

## Rond de Jambe

### Purpose of the Resistance Band

The purpose and use of the resistance band in this exercise is similar to that of the battement tendus from fifth position, and provides students another opportunity to explore the use of the torso as a connector for the entire body. The band is held in a hand-to-foot hold, and as the working leg passes through each circle, the torso counterbalances by rotating in the opposite direction to the leg. For example, as the right leg circles en dehors, the torso will rotate to the left, and then back to the right again as the leg passes through first position.

Though this exercise provides an excellent opportunity for students to explore further the engagement of the torso, I will often provide students with a choice: they can either choose to use the band in a hand-to-foot hold as I have described above, or they can use the band in a back hold to explore the sense of stability and length in the upper body as found in the battement dégagés. I encourage them to choose based upon their experiences and discoveries so far and what has proved to be most useful for them.

The description and figures below use the band in a hand-to-foot hold, as the back hold is more self-explanatory.

### Sample Phrase

Begins in fifth position croisé, right foot devant, arms in second position with the band in a hand-to-foot hold (Figure 28). The loop of the resistance band is around the right arch, and the end of the band is held in the right hand with some tension to start.

| Count | 1 | 2 | 3 | 4 |
|---|---|---|---|---|
| Movement | Tendu devant (Figure 29) | Demi-rond de jambe to écarté devant (Figure 30) | Demi-rond de jambe to tendu derriére (Figure 31) | Close to first position (Figure 32) |

| 5 - 8 | 1 | 2 | and |
|---|---|---|---|
| Repeat the previous 4 counts | Tendu devant | Rond de jambe to tendu derriére | Brush through first position |

| 3 - 4 | 5 - 7 | 8 |
|---|---|---|
| Repeat the previous 2 counts | Rond de jambe en l'air en dehors (Figures 33-35) | Close in fifth position effacé (Figure 36) |

The 16 counts above are reversed (beginning with tendu derriére). Then there are 8 counts in which to switch the band to the other foot and prepare for the other side (beginning croisé with the left foot devant).

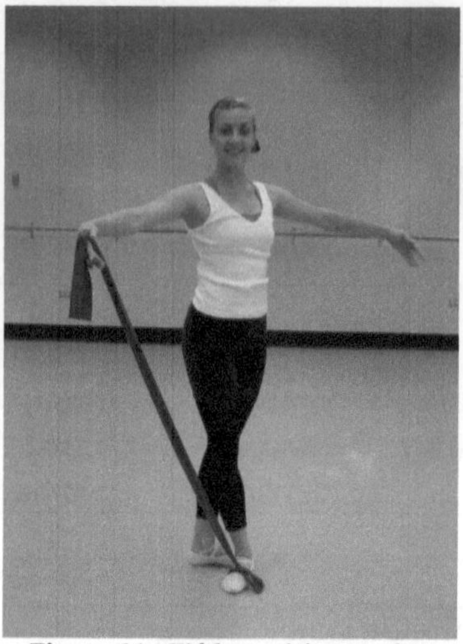
Figure 28. Fifth position croisé

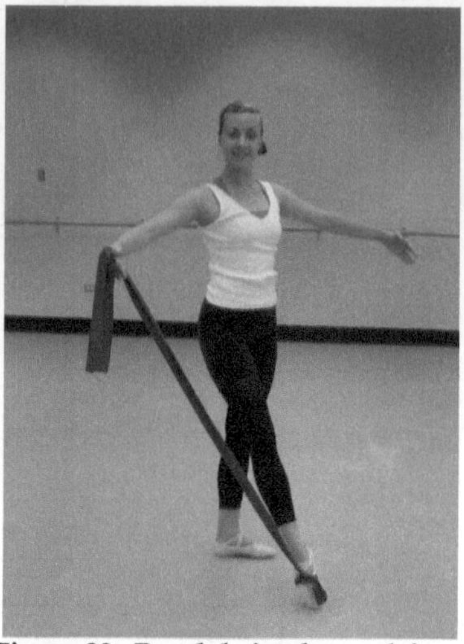
Figure 29. Rond de jambe en dehors

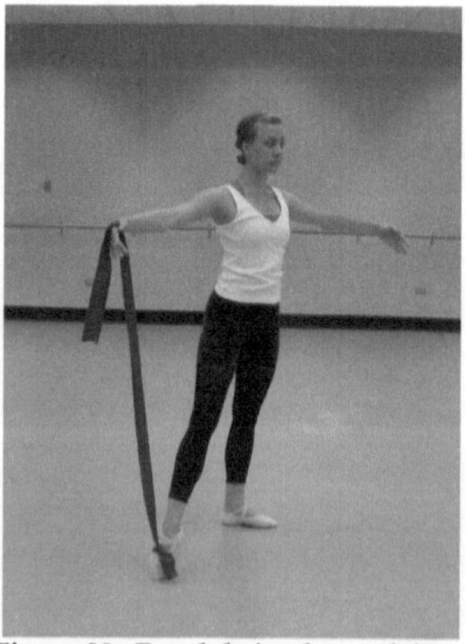
Figure 30. Rond de jambe en dehors

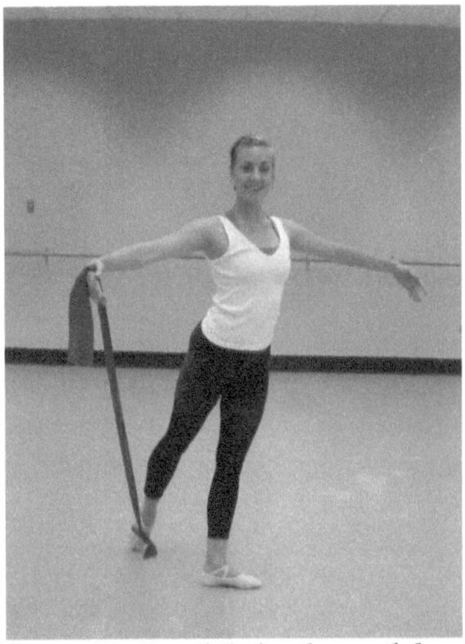

Figure 31. Rond de jambe en dehors

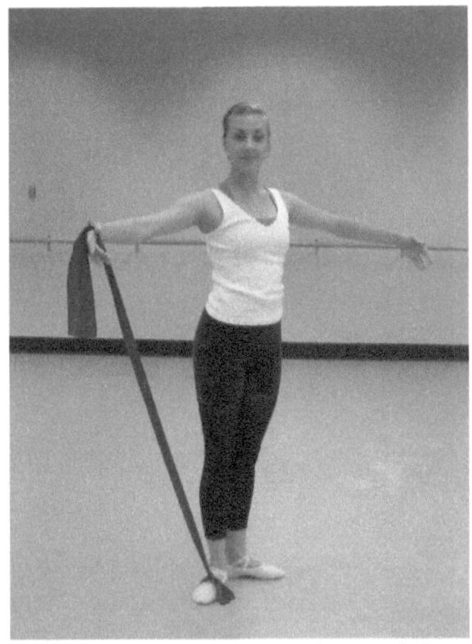

Figure 32. Rond de jambe en dehors

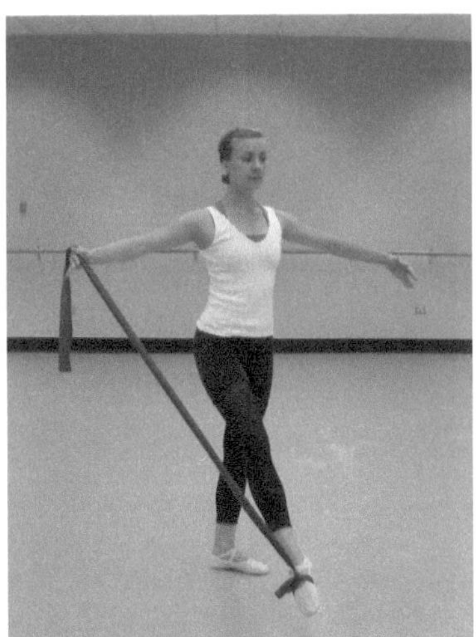

Figure 33. Rond de jambe en l'air

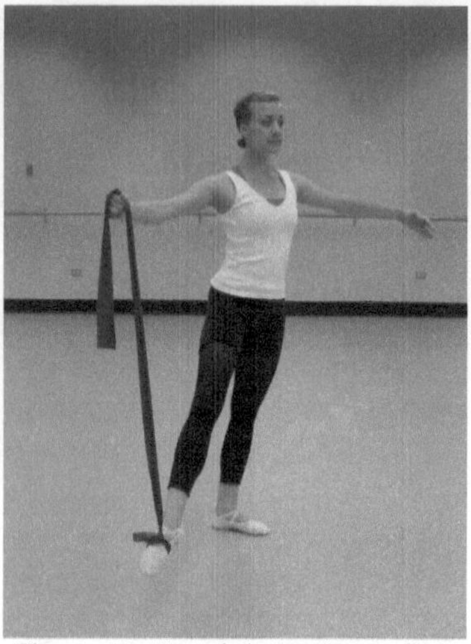
Figure 34. Rond de jambe en l'air

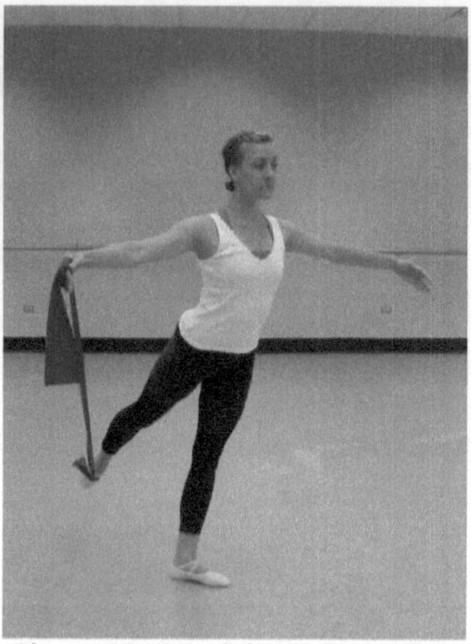
Figure 35. Rond de jambe en l'air

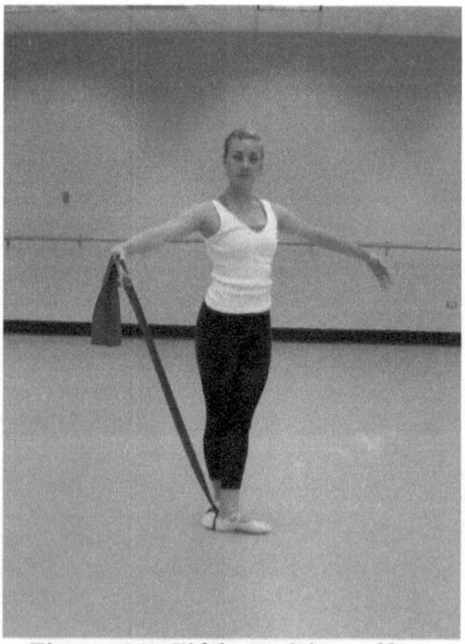
Figure 36. Fifth position effacé

As with the battement tendus from fifth position, I will encourage students to exaggerate the rotation of the torso to counter the leg. Such rotation in rond de jambe en l'air would look like the following (devant and derriére):

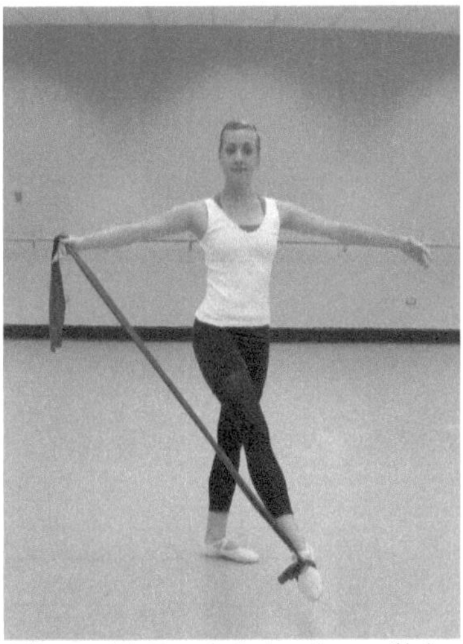

**Figure 37. Rond de jambe en l'air, emphasizing rotation of the torso**

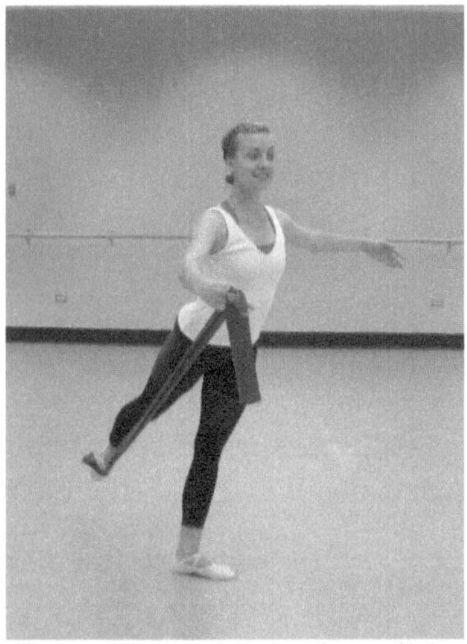

**Figure 38. Rond de jambe en l'air, emphasizing rotation of the torso**

## Battement Fondu

### Purpose of the Resistance Band

During battement fondus, as during pliés and battement tendus, the upper body is often forgotten as the focus turns to the movement of the legs. However, the upper body is of extreme importance not only in providing stability for the body, but in allowing the entire body to be used as a whole. The use of the resistance band here is similar to its use during battement tendus from first position, with the band in a back hold. As the arms remain in second position, they are encouraged by the band to remain active and lengthened, while remaining connected to and supported by the upper back.

### Sample Phrase

Begins in fifth position en face, right foot devant, arms in second position, band in a back hold.

| Count | 1 – 2 | 3 | 4 | 5 – 8 and 1 – 8 |
|---|---|---|---|---|
| Movement | Fondu devant (Figures 39 & 40) | Élevé on the left leg, arms remain in second (Figure 41) | Lower the left heel, arms remain in second (Figure 42) | Repeat en croix, with the right leg closing to fifth derriére after the last repetition |

These 16 counts are then repeated on the left side. Students are encouraged to feel an even greater sense of reach and energy through the arms each time they élevé. Though I usually have students leave their arms in second position, they can also explore moving the arms from first to second position in a slightly more traditional pathway during the battement fondu.

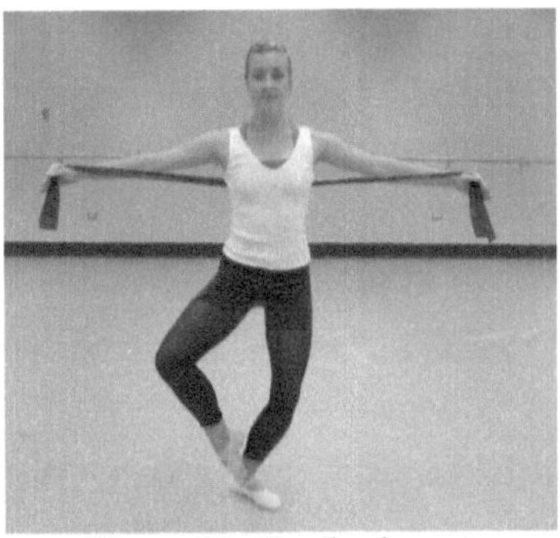

Figure 39. Fondu devant

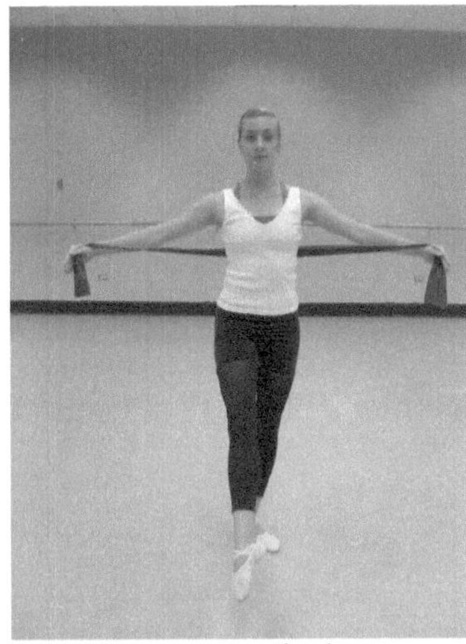

Figure 40. Fondu devant

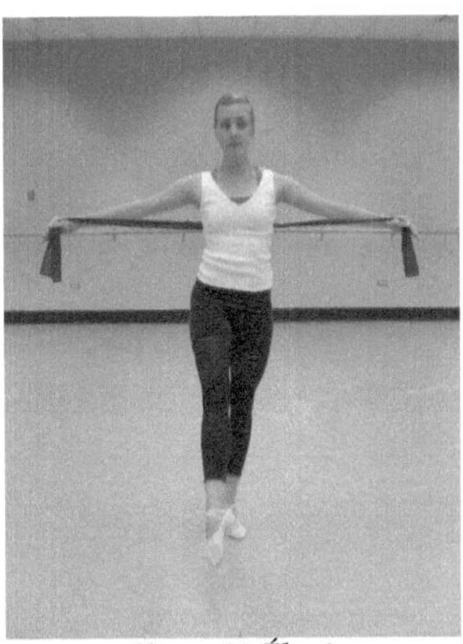

Figure 41. Élevé

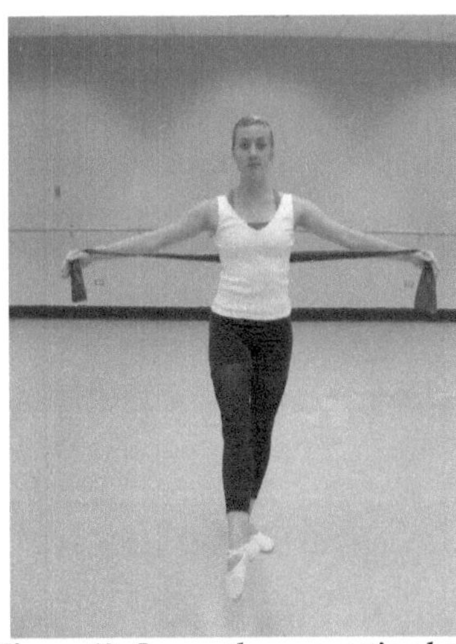

Figure 42. Lower the supporting heel

## Battement Frappé

### Purpose of the Resistance Band

In battement frappés, as in battement dégagés, students often neglect the upper body or fail to connect the arms in a way that provides stability and creates energy and length. As the movements of the legs become faster, the arms and upper body can be extremely helpful in supporting the torso. In this exercise, the band is held in a back hold to generate that stability while also encouraging a sense of length throughout the entire body.

### Sample Phrase

Begins en face, right foot in fifth position devant, arms in second position with the band in a back hold. If I am teaching a new group of students, I tell them to perform whichever method of battement frappés they are used to (using a flexed foot, or sur le cou-de-pied).

| Count | 7 – 8 | 1 | 2 |
|---|---|---|---|
| Movement | Tendu à la seconde, bring the foot to sur le cou-de-pied (or a flexed position) devant to prepare (Figure 43) | Frappé devant (Figure 44) | Frappé devant |

| 3 & 4 | 5 – 8, 1 – 8 |
|---|---|
| 3 quicker frappés devant | Repeat en croix, excluding the last 3 quick frappés. Instead the right foot will close fifth position derriére, and the left foot will prepare. |

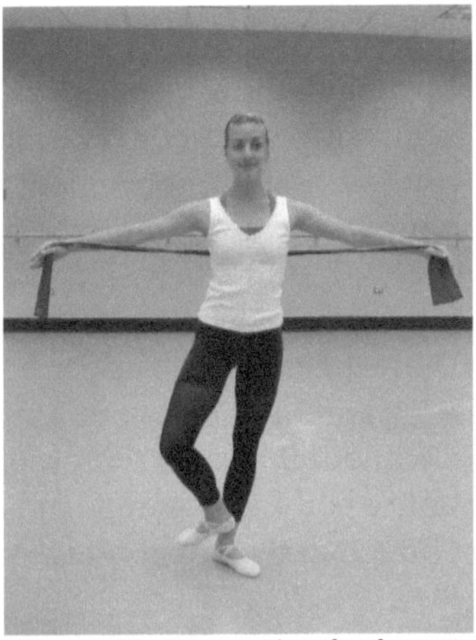

Figure 43. Preparation for frappé

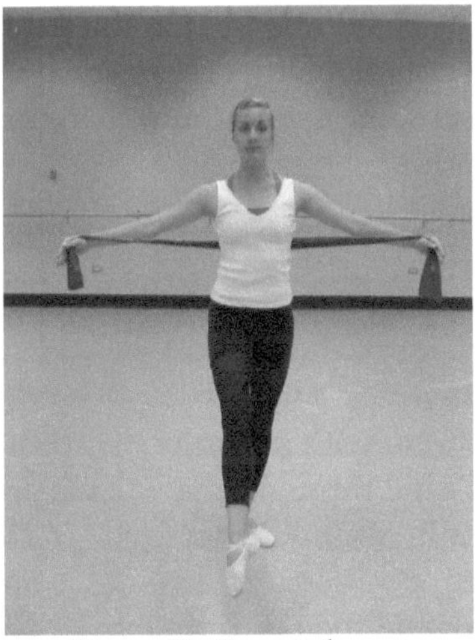

Figure 44. Frappé devant

## Développé

### Purpose of the Resistance Band

In développés, though the arms and legs may appear to be coordinated, there is often little sense or understanding in students of how the upper body assists in the movement by providing stability, muscular connections, and counterbalancing. By using the band in a hand-to-foot hold, students will have physical, tangible connections between these very distal parts of their bodies. They will be able to sense how the use of the upper body with the band literally helps lift the leg and provide a counterbalance. When repeating the phrase without the band, their sense of understanding will encompass the entire body as one unit, and the movement itself may even feel easier now that the upper body is appropriately utilized.

### Sample Phrase

Begins en face, with the right foot in fifth position devant. The band is used in a hand-to-foot hold, with the loop around the right arch, and the opposite end held in the left hand to start. There may not be tension initially, but once movement begins, students should be able to feel some tension, and therefore some connection, throughout the développé.

| Count | 1 - 8 | 1 - 8 |
|---|---|---|
| Movement | Right leg performs a développé devant and then closes to fifth position, with the arms moving through first (middle fifth) position to fourth position (left arm high), and then lowering to en bas (Figure 45-47) | Right leg performs a développé à la seconde and then closes to fifth position derriére, with the arms moving through first position and opening to second position, and then lowering to en bas (Figure 48) |

| & | 1 - 8 | 1 - 8 |
|---|---|---|
| Switch band to right hand | Right leg performs a développé derriére and closes to fifth position, with the arms moving through first position to second arabesque (right arm reaches forward), and then lowering to en bas (Figures 49-52) | Switch band to left foot and right hand, and prepare to repeat on the other side |

**Additional Information and Suggestions**

- Throughout this exercise, students are encouraged to feel how the upper body is literally lifting and helping to hold the extended leg.

- For the développé à la seconde in particular, timing is critical, as the left arm and right leg must extend together to correctly counterbalance each other.

- During the développé derriére, students must ensure that their legs are extending directly behind them, and their extended arms reaching directly forward. In this manner, they can feel a direct sense of reach and length between the lifted arm and leg. Also, students are encouraged to find the sense of torso rotation they explored earlier in rond de jambes to help them sense this reach in arabesque. More specifically, the right ribs should rotate forwards to allow the right arm to reach more fully, while the right leg and hip are lengthening to the back.

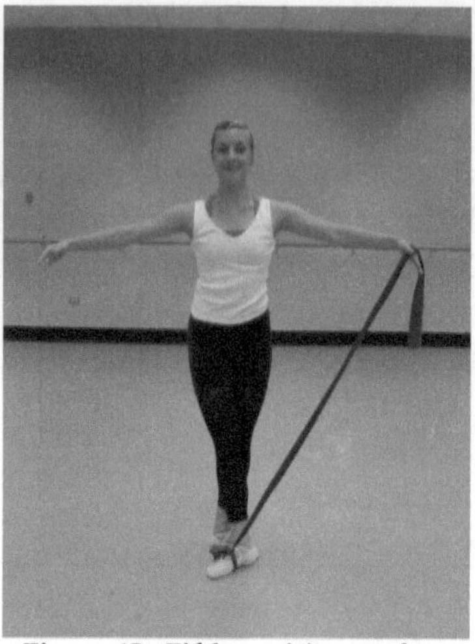

Figure 45. Fifth position en face

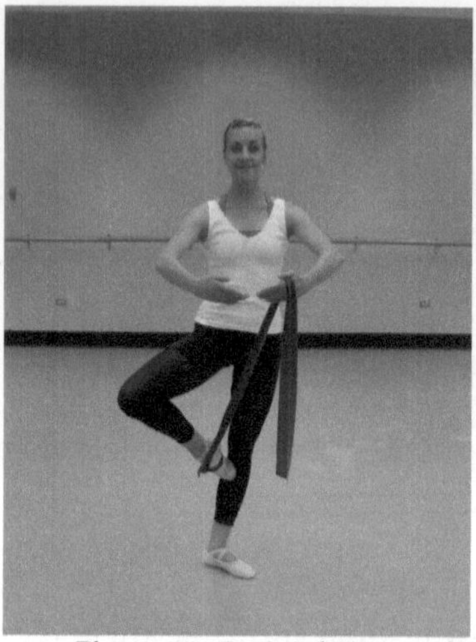

Figure 46. Retiré devant

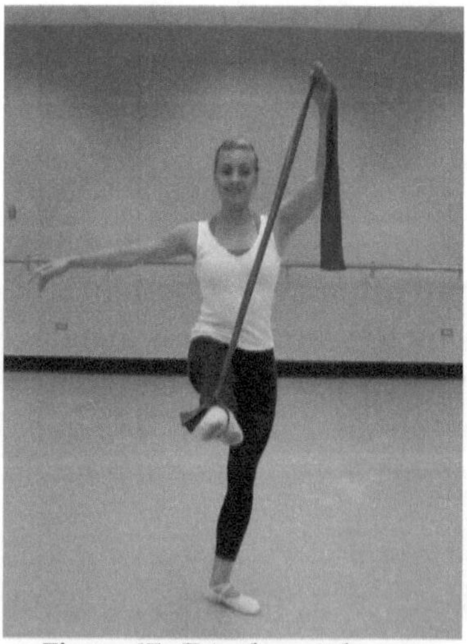

Figure 47. Développé devant

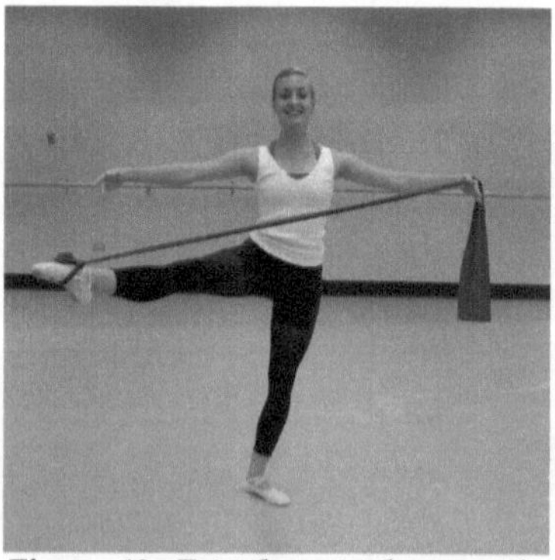

Figure 48. Développé à la seconde

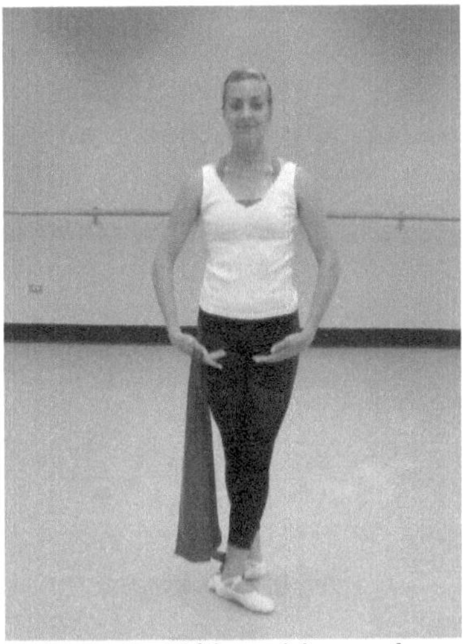
Figure 49. Fifth position en face

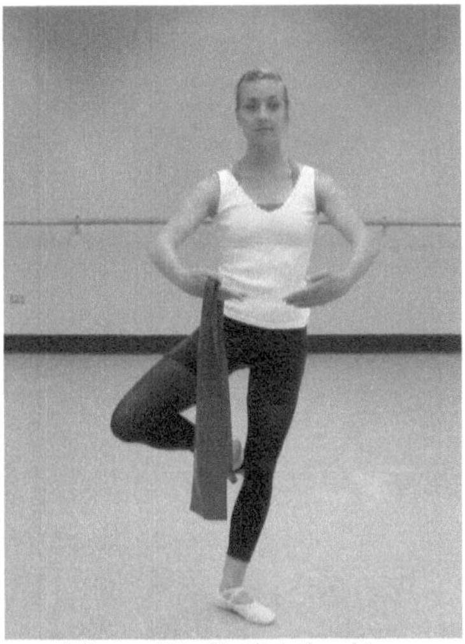
Figure 50. Retiré derriére

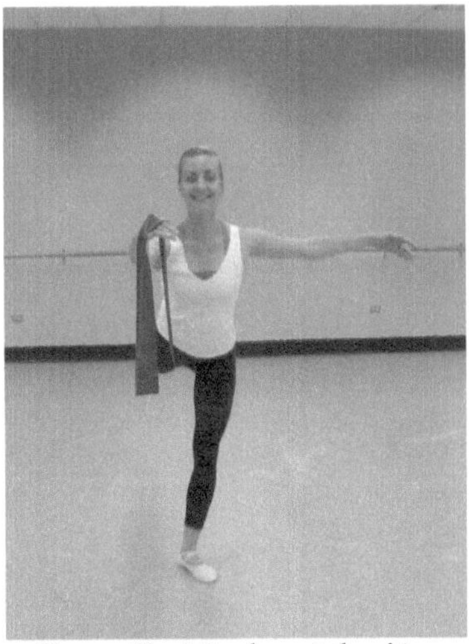
Figure 51. Développé derriére

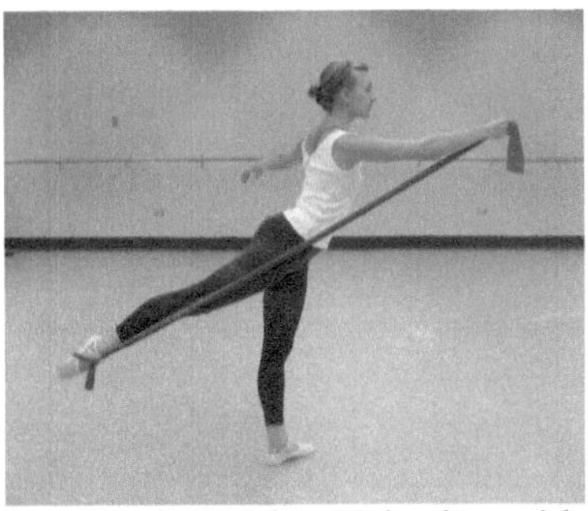
Figure 52. Développé derriére, side view

## Grand Battement

### Purpose of the Resistance Band

The use of the resistance band for grand battements is similar to that for battement dégagés and battement frappés. There is often a focus on the legs during grand battements, and students then neglect the role of the upper body in producing and supporting this movement. In using the band in a back hold, students can explore the stability that the band helps them create. In addition, given that grand battements are much larger movements than battement frappés, for example, there will be much more counterbalancing that needs to occur within the upper body. Through use of the band, students will be more aware of this counterbalancing and how critical it is to complete the movement successfully and efficiently.

### Sample Phrase

Begins en face, right foot in fifth position devant. Arms are in second position with the band in a back hold, and remain in second position throughout the entire exercise.

| Count | 1 - 5 | 6 | 7 - 8 |
|---|---|---|---|
| Movement | Grand battement en cloche in attitude with the right leg, beginning and ending to the front (Figures 53 & 54) | Close fifth position devant | Demi plié, soussus (Figures 55 & 56) |

| 1 - 6 | 7 - 8 | 1 - 6 |
|---|---|---|
| 3 grand battements devant on demi-pointe (Figure 57) | Demi plié, soussus | 3 grand battements à la seconde on demi-pointe, ending right foot derriére (Figure 58) |

| 7 - 8 | 1 - 6 | 7 - 8 |
|---|---|---|
| Demi plié, soussus | 3 grand battements derriére on demi-pointe (Figure 59) | Demi plié, prepare to repeat on left side |

**Additional Information and Suggestions**

- During the grand battements à la seconde, students are encouraged to feel the opposite hand reaching during the movement; as the right leg performs the grand battement, the left hand should reach out a bit more than the right to counter balance and help keep the body centered.

- During the grand battements derriére, students are reminded of the shift of the upper body slightly forward to counterbalance as the leg lifts, and then the returning of the body to vertical as the leg lowers.

- Performing this exercise on demi-pointe challenges students' stability and encourages them to become more aware of how their entire body is moving and working together to achieve dynamic balance. I have used this exercise as is with beginning students (after approximately 8 weeks of a college class) as well as with advanced students.

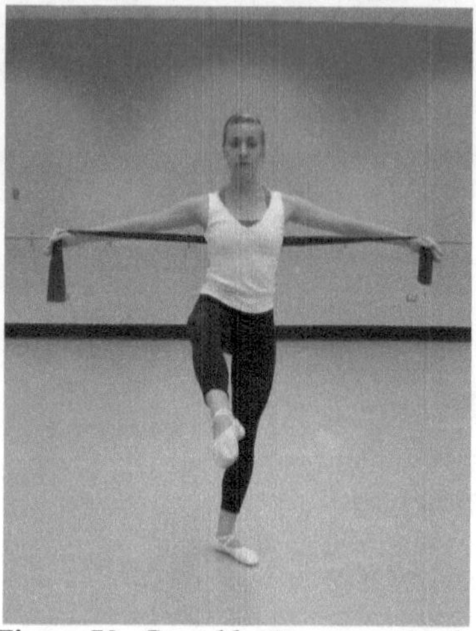

Figure 53. Grand battement attitude devant

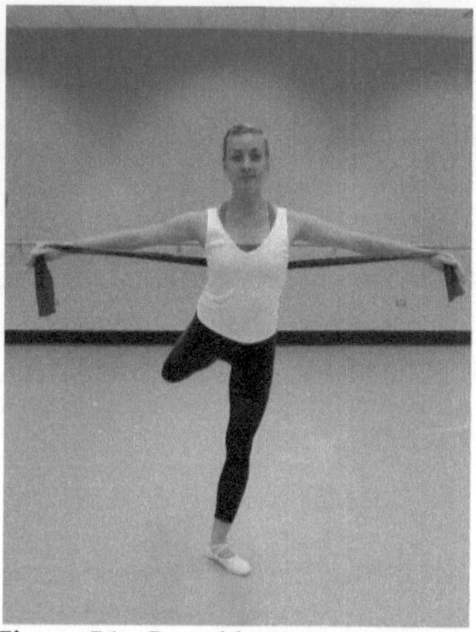

Figure 54. Grand battement attitude derriére

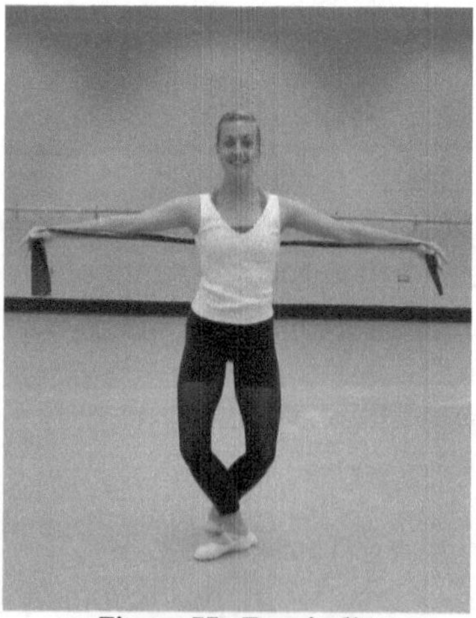

Figure 55. Demi plié

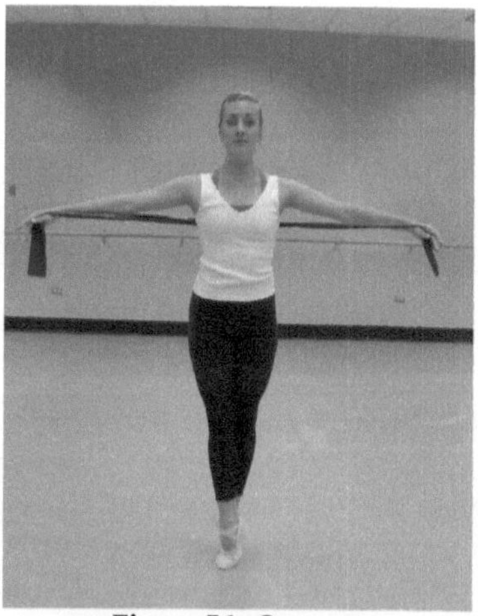

Figure 56. Soussus

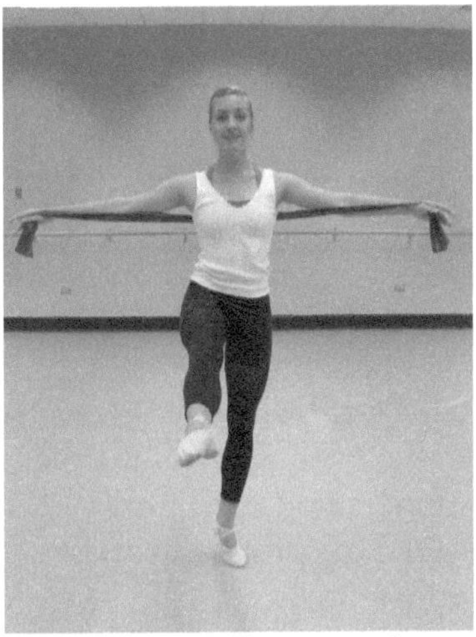

Figure 57. Grand battement devant on demi-pointe

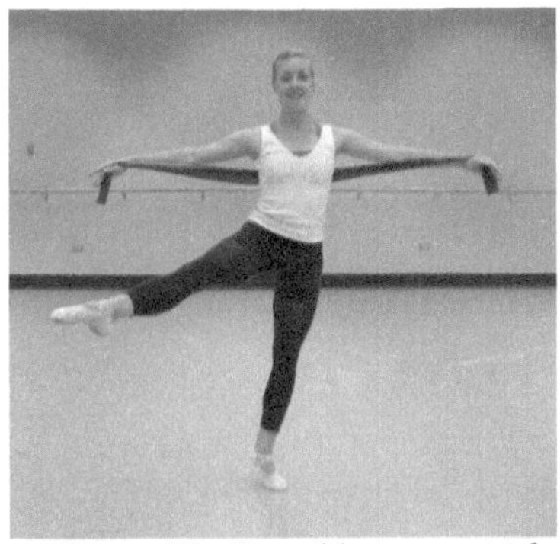

Figure 58. Grand battement à la seconde

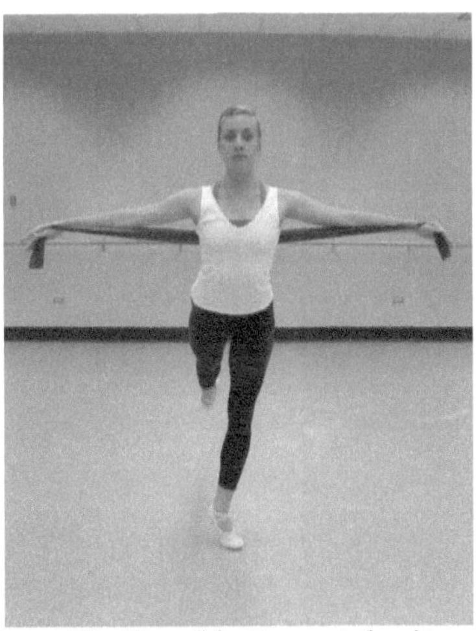

Figure 59. Grand battement derriére on demi-pointe

# Pirouette En Dehors from Fifth Position

## Purpose of the Resistance Band

In pirouettes en dehors from fifth position, we often talk about the entire body moving as one piece, feeling the knee of the lifted leg pulling us around, and feeling arms connecting to the body. However, for some students these sensations may be hard to sense kinesthetically, even if they make sense mentally. For this exercise, the band is looped around the thigh of the lifted leg, and the other end is held by the contralateral hand; thus, there is a physical connection between the two halves of the body. As one turns, so must the other, and the idea of the bent knee pulling the rest of the body around is more easily understood. The turns become more smooth and solid, rather than the piecemeal and disconnected turns we may often see from students.

## Sample Phrase

Begins in fifth position en face, right foot devant (Figure 60). The band is wrapped around the right thigh just above the knee, with the end pulled through the loop, like a noose (Figure 61). The opposite end is held by the left hand. The arms remain in first (middle fifth) position throughout the exercise, with tension between the left hand and right knee at all times (even when the feet are in fifth position).

I usually use a slow tempo for this phrase, to allow students the opportunity to fully sense the connections present in each position and movement.

| Count | 1 - 2 | 3 - 4 | 5 - 8 |
|---|---|---|---|
| Movement | Demi plié (Figure 62) | Straighten the left leg while the right leg lifts to retiré devant (Figure 63) | Repeat the previous 4 counts |

| 1 - 2 | 3 - 4 | 5 - 8 |
|---|---|---|
| Demi plié | Relevé to retiré devant | Repeat the previous 4 counts |

| 1 - 2 | 3 - 4 | 5 - 8, 1 - 8 |
|---|---|---|
| Demi plié | Relevé to retiré devant with a quarter turn en dehors | Repeat the previous 4 counts 3 more times, ending en face |

| 1 - 2 | 3 - 4 | 5 - 8 |
|---|---|---|
| Demi plié | Relevé to retiré devant with a half turn en dehors | Repeat the previous 4 counts, ending en face |

| 1 - 2 | 3 - 4 | 5 - 8 |
|---|---|---|
| Demi plié | Relevé to retiré devant with a full pirouette en dehors (if desired) | Repeat the previous 4 counts (if desired) |

The entire phrase is then repeated on the left side. I may or may not have students attempt the full pirouette, depending on their experiences with the first part of the exercise. More repetitions of each movement, before advancing to the next, have also been helpful to the students.

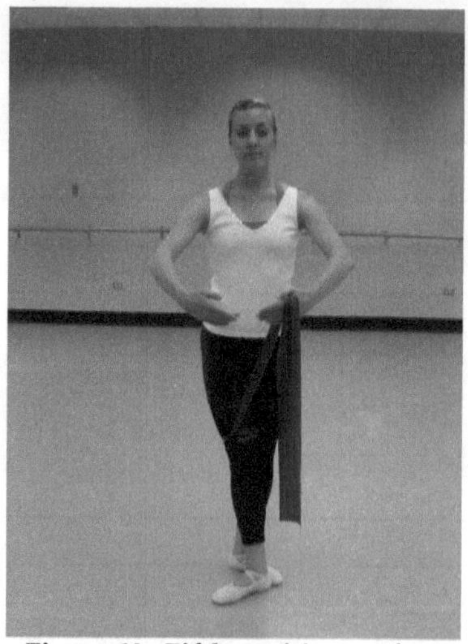

**Figure 60. Fifth position en face**

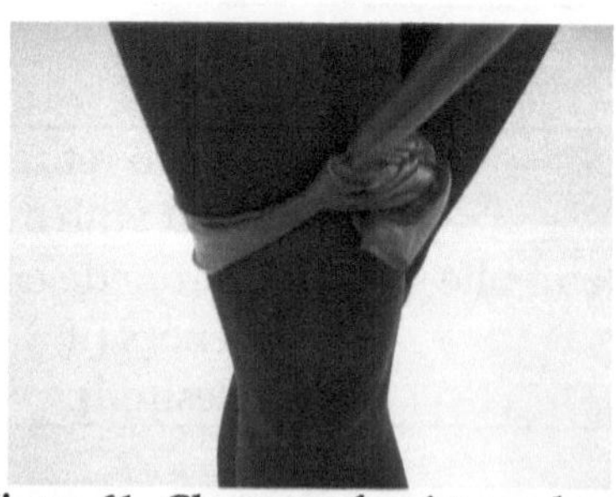

**Figure 61. Close-up of resistance band**

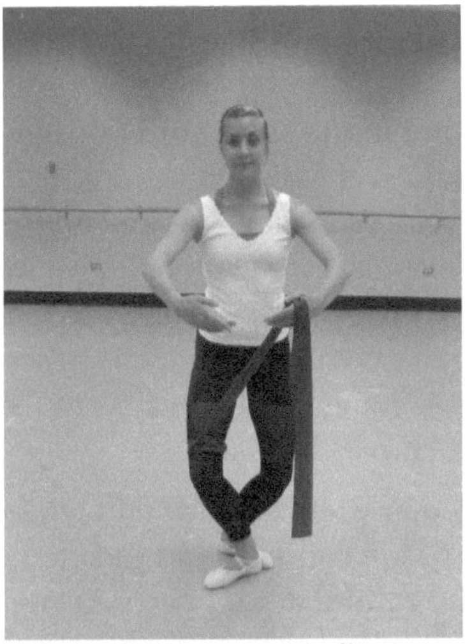

Figure 62. Demi plié

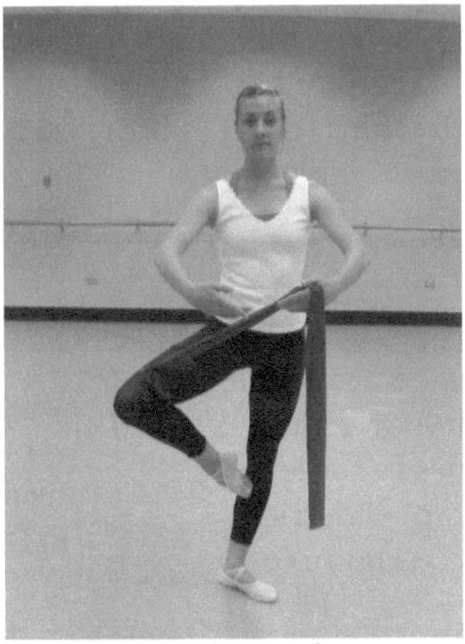

Figure 63. Retiré devant

# Adagio

## Purpose of the Resistance Band

Until this point in the class, students have used the resistance band in relatively static positions; though the limbs may be moving, the movement itself is not much larger than a simple développé. In this exercise, we explore larger movement in an adagio. Students are encouraged not only to feel the connections present in the body in given positions, but to sense how these dynamic connections change and adjust as the body shifts to a different position or moves in space.

In this particular exercise, the band is used in a hand-to-foot hold, with one end of the band around the arch of the foot, and the other end held in the contralateral hand. As opposed to the développé exercise in which the band crosses in front of the body, here the band passes behind the body, as we will see below.

## Sample Phrase

Begins fifth position croisé, right foot devant (Figure 64). The loop of the band is around the left foot, and the other end passes in between the shins (while in fifth position), and is held in the right hand (Figure 65).

| Count | 1 | 2 - 8 |
|---|---|---|
| Movement | Step en avant onto the right foot as the left foot comes to sur le cou-de-pied derriére (Figure 66) | Développé derriére with the left leg, finishing in attitude derriére. Arms pass through first position, and then move to fourth position (left arm high). (Figures 67 & 68) |

| 1 – 8 | 1 – 4 |
|---|---|
| Promenade en dedans in attitude derriére, ending effacé derriére (one-and-a-quarter turns) (Figure 69) | Fondu in first arabesque (Figure 70) |

| 5 – 7 | 8 | 1 – 8 |
|---|---|---|
| Lower to tendu effacé derriére, as right leg straightens (Figure 71) | Close to fifth position effacé (Figure 72) | Prepare to repeat on the other side |

When repeating this phrase without the resistance band, rather than closing the leg into fifth position effacé to finish the side, brush the leg en cloche and close into fifth position croisé devant. Then demi plié, soussus, and hold, before lowering to repeat on the second side.

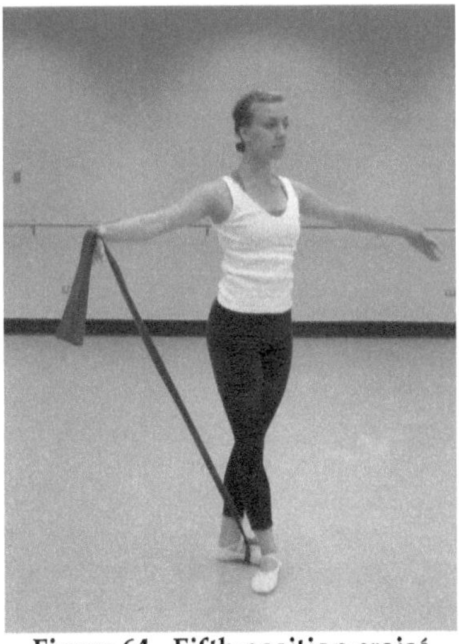

**Figure 64. Fifth position croisé devant**

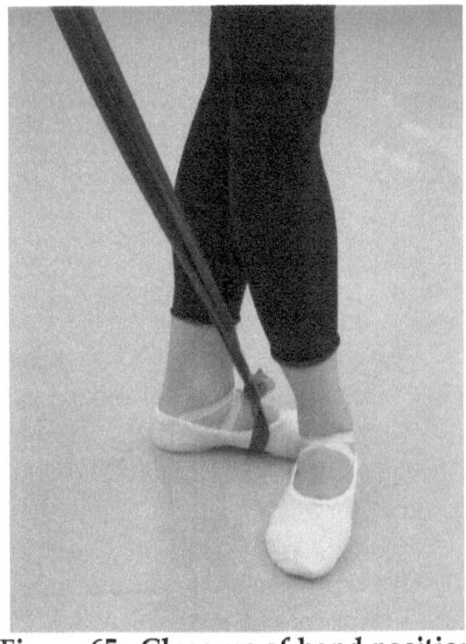

**Figure 65. Close-up of band position**

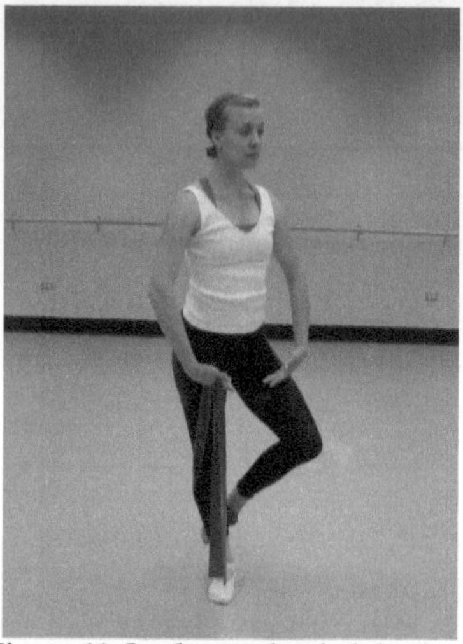

Figure 66. Sur le cou-de-pied derriére

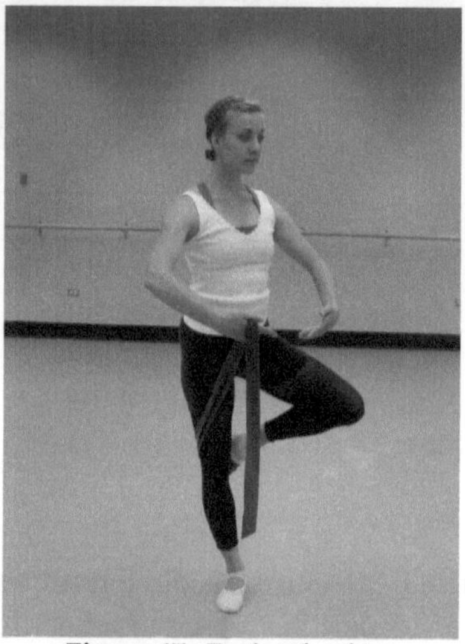

Figure 67. Retiré derriére

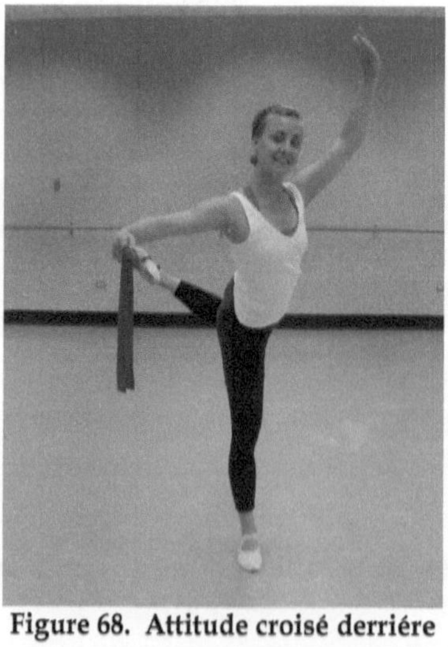

Figure 68. Attitude croisé derriére

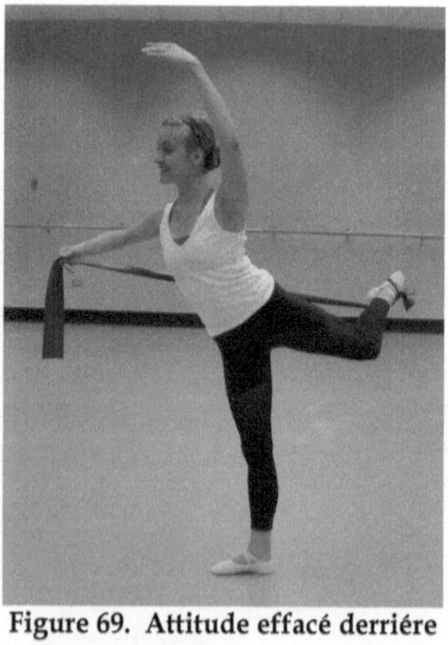

Figure 69. Attitude effacé derriére

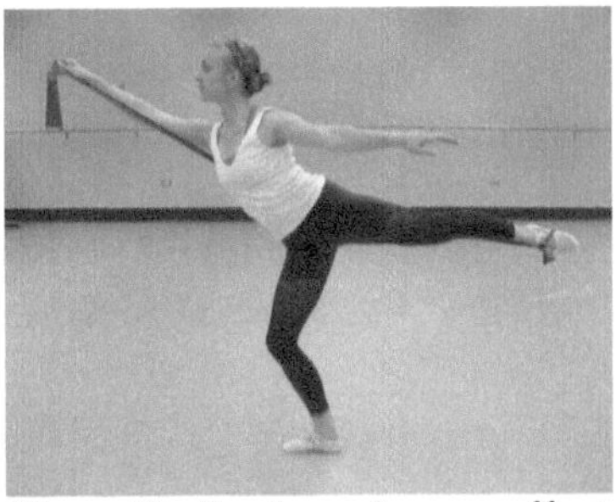
Figure 70. Fondu arabesque effacé

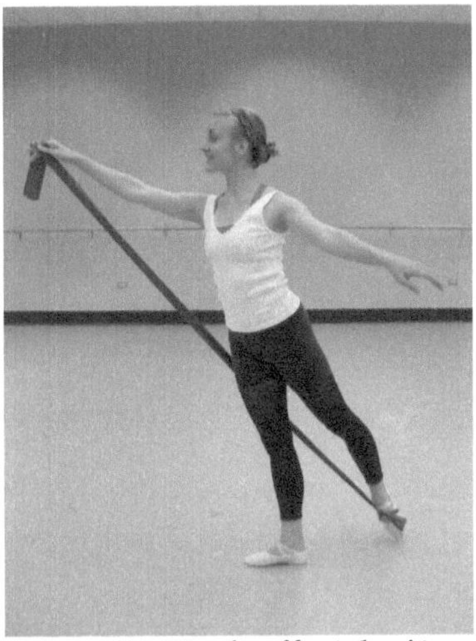
Figure 71. Tendu effacé derriére

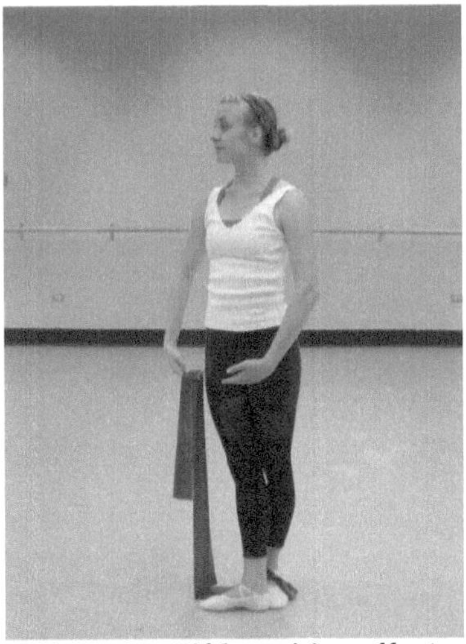
Figure 72. Fifth position effacé

## Other Ideas

In exploring the myriad of uses of the resistance band, I have come across two other instances that have consistently given students a better understanding of their movement.

- *Chaînés*
  I will have the students use the band in either a front hold or a back hold while performing chaînés, and I allow them to choose which hold feels most beneficial. In using the band in this way, students suddenly become much more aware of how/if the arms and upper body are moving simultaneously with the lower body as it rotates. When repeated without the band, students' turns look much more smooth and synchronized.

- *Balancing*
  The resistance band can be useful in any type of balance on demi-pointe or flat. Depending on the position of the body, the band can be used in a variety of ways to emphasize desired connections between different areas of the body, and to encourage length and energy throughout. Students then become more aware of these ideas as they rise to demi-pointe and continue to balance. In addition, students often become more aware of the dynamic counterbalancing that must continue to function within the balance.

Though I usually run out of class time after all of the previous exercises, there are certainly many other ways in which the resistance band can be used to explore technical ideas and provide students with greater insights into their movement. Feel free to explore and find what helps your students the most!

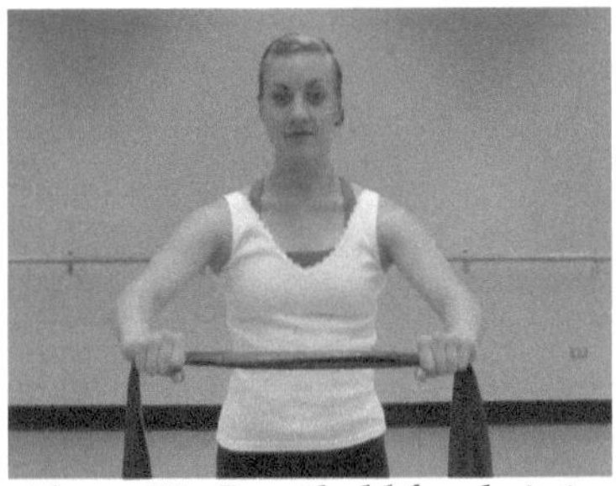
Figure 73. Front hold for chaînés

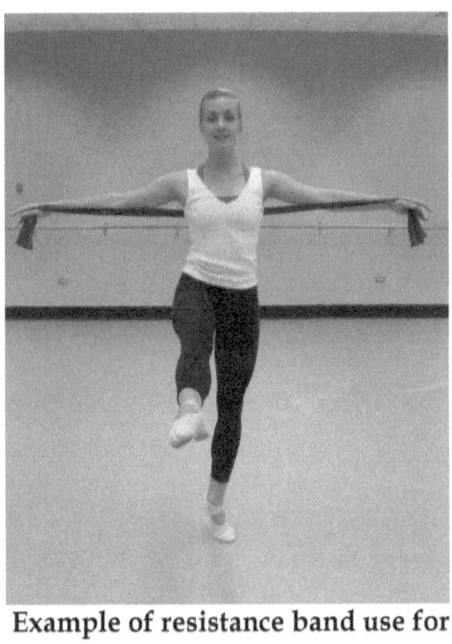
Figure 74. Example of resistance band use for balancing

## Acknowledgements

For introducing me to a new approach to ballet, I would like to thank Dr. Cynthia Roses-Thema, whose classes completely changed my dancing and teaching. I would also like to thank Jenna Kosowski for her initial inspiration and constant, always appreciated, feedback. For her consent to be photographed, I would like to thank Whitney Hancock. This booklet would never have been written (or would have been written five years later) had it not been for Angela Rosenkrans, whom I am fortunate enough to consider a friend, mentor, and ardent supporter of everything I do.

## Biography of Author

After temporarily leaving dance to receive her BS in Mathematics with a minor in Chemistry from the University of Puget Sound in 2002, Lisa returned to the art form and began searching for a way to combine her two passions, science and dance. She took numerous courses in anatomy and kinesiology to further her knowledge of these subjects, and she applied this knowledge while working at a physical therapy clinic, and later while in graduate school. After receiving her MFA in Dance from Arizona State University in 2008, Lisa decided to pursue her certification in Pilates. She completed her training with a dance specialization with Karen Clippinger through Body Arts and Science International in 2008.

Currently, Lisa is Adjunct Faculty in Dance and Co-Artistic Director of SCC Moving Company at Scottsdale Community College (SCC) in Scottsdale, AZ; Adjunct Faculty in Dance at Grand Canyon University in Phoenix, AZ; and she also teaches Pilates in Phoenix. Lisa has taught ballet, modern, tap, dance kinesiology, dance conditioning, and Pilates for Dancers at the college level, along with developing curricula and course materials for several SCC courses, and she has received recognition from faculty and students alike for her teaching. Lisa is currently serving as the Co-Treasurer for the Arizona Dance Education Organization, and she has also presented on the teaching of dance technique at the National Dance Education Organization's 2006, 2008 and 2010 national conferences.

For more information, or to contact Lisa with questions or master class requests, please visit www.lisathorngren.com

www.ingramcontent.com/pod-product-compliance
Lightning Source LLC
Chambersburg PA
CBHW021911170526
45157CB00005B/2042
* 9 7 8 1 2 5 7 9 9 6 7 2 8 *